FIERCE
MARRIAGE
PARTICIPANT'S GUIDE

D1529107

FIERCE MARRIAGE

PARTICIPANT'S GUIDE

*RADICALLY PURSUING
EACH OTHER IN LIGHT OF
CHRIST'S RELENTLESS LOVE*

RYAN *AND* SELENA FREDERICK

BakerBooks
a division of Baker Publishing Group
Grand Rapids, Michigan

Published by Baker Books
a division of Baker Publishing Group
PO Box 6287, Grand Rapids, MI 49516-6287
www.bakerbooks.com

Printed in the United States of America

ISBN 978-0-8010-9390-6

The authors are represented by Alive Literary Agency, 7680 Goddard Street, Suite 200, Colorado Springs, CO 80920, www.aliveliterary.com.

18   19   20   21   22   23   24   7   6   5   4   3   2   1

Contents

Introduction

This isn't your typical marriage video series. At least we don't think it is. In our experience, there are many valuable resources about marriage, particularly in modern Christendom. But we've observed that videos in the Christian marriage category tend to fall on either side of what we call the hopeful-helpful intersection, which is sometimes problematic. Here's what we mean.

Hopeful videos offer what we need for eternal hope: reminders of the gospel, deep explorations of scriptural truth, and theologically rich prose. While these are incredible, they can leave us wondering where we should go from here. Our hearts and heads are filled, but our hands are left wondering what's next. The viewer is charged with discovering the particulars of how to apply their newfound knowledge.

Helpful video series are the inverse. They offer plenty of practical advice—action steps—without troubling too much with the underlying theological truths behind them. The tragedy with these is that viewers rarely learn the reasons behind the actions they take. We hear what to do without understanding why we are doing it—not truly, anyway. Our behavior changes for a time, but our beliefs are largely unaffected. In our years of speaking with and ministering to married couples, this has proven troublesome.

We wanted to create a video series that was different. If we were going to add another series to the Christian marriage stockpile, we wanted it all. We wanted something that infused viewers with deep, beautiful, eternal gospel truth while equipping them with time-tested, wisdom-fueled advice for how to apply it. In short, we envisioned a video series that could meet viewers at the intersection of hopeful and helpful.

Fierce Marriage is our attempt at exactly that. It's our "marriage manifesto." Our modern tell-all. An exposé revealing all we believe marriage can be according to the Bible. We've done the exegesis of Scripture, read the commentaries, compiled the research, and done our absolute best to synthesize gospel-centered help that is rooted in the never-failing hope of Christ. We've worked hard to discern how much to expect from you, how much you should expect from us, and what you can expect to have once you finish this video series.

We made a decision early on to expect much from you, dear viewer. We expect that you want to know more than just a few new techniques for helping your marriage. We expect that you want to grow deeper in your understanding of Scripture and how it applies to your marriage. And we expect that you want to learn to trust Jesus more—with your heart and your spouse's heart.

From us, you can expect our best work. You can expect honesty. We've shared stories that you will most likely never hear elsewhere— they're the stories we'd tell you if we had dinner together. They're stories of pain, joy, romance, anger, and deep conviction. We've shared them all here, hopefully for your benefit. Finally, and most of all, you can expect from us a heavy reliance on Scripture and commitment to what it says.

Now, from this video series you can also expect order with a heavy dose of levity. What follows is a distillation of ideas that have been passed through layer after layer of theological and editorial oversight. We're not theologians in the scholarly sense, so we have asked smarter men and women than us to keep us in line. The end result, we hope, is a clear understanding of scriptural truths and how those truths affect and transform our marriage.

The sessions in the video series are intentionally organized to be hopeful first and helpful second. We will start in session 1 by sharing a key event in our lives and marriage that has forever shaped us. Session 2 describes the magnitude of the marriage covenant. Session 3 focuses on priorities and finances. Session 4 covers communication and conflict. Session 5 looks at intimacy and sex. Finally, session 6 casts a vision for what can be had in a fierce marriage and extends an invitation to those who will have it. In order to get the most out of the video series, we urge you to read the corresponding chapters in the book as you go.

While we don't know everything, we promise to share what we do know honestly. We're not counselors or ordained ministers, nor do we claim to have all the answers. All we have is Jesus and more than half our lives together, and all we can do is talk about what he's done. We do know one thing for sure: we wouldn't be married today if it weren't for the loving-kindness and infinite grace of Christ.

Finally, thank you. Thank you for inviting us into your life as you watch the video series. And thank you for allowing us to speak into your marriage, your most sacred and personal relationship. We hope and pray that this video series blesses you and your marriage for years to come.

Stay fierce,

Ryan and Selena

Our Swiss Adventure

The Early Years

Before watching Session 1 of the DVD,
read chapters 1–2 of *Fierce Marriage*.

WATCH SESSION 1

Video Notes

As you watch the video, use the following space to take notes.

_____

_____

_____

_____

_____

_____

_____

_____

_____

_____

_____

_____

_____

_____

_____

_____

_____

_____

_____

_____

Discussion Questions

> Pain insists upon being attended to. God whispers to us in our pleasures, speaks in our consciences, but shouts in our pains. It is his megaphone to rouse a deaf world.
>
> C. S. Lewis

1. Many couples go into marriage thinking that their relationship will be problem-free. Why is this an unrealistic expectation in light of the gospel's diagnosis?

   _____

   _____

   _____

   _____

2. Since both marriage partners are sinners, why is it so important that we give grace to and receive grace from each other?

   _____

   _____

   _____

   _____

3. Reread the C. S. Lewis quote above. How can the Lord use conflicts and difficulties in marriage to sanctify us and to draw us closer to each other and to him?

   _____

   _____

   _____

   _____

4. In what ways is Christ's death on the cross a personification of God's love?

_____

_____

_____

_____

_____

5. How should Christ's example of love transform the way we view and practice love in the marriage relationship?

_____

_____

_____

_____

_____

_____

6. How does everything in marriage flow out of the gospel, including communicating well, extending grace, and forgiving each other?

_____

_____

_____

_____

_____

7. Ryan's sickness and surgery opened his and Selena's eyes to why they needed Jesus in their marriage. How have hardships and difficulties heightened your need for Jesus in your marriage relationship?

_____

_____

_____

_____

_____

8. Almost seven years to the day after surgery, Ryan was finally able to climb Mount Rainier. In a similar way, why do you think the gospel's recovery process in our lives takes so much time?

_____

_____

_____

_____

For Personal Reflection

- On a scale of 0 to 10, how much is Jesus / the gospel involved in your marriage?

0	1	2	3	4	5	6	7	8	9	10

Not at all   Jesus is the center

17

- Why did you choose the number you did?

_____

_____

_____

_____

- How have you tried to improve your marriage in the past?

_____

_____

_____

_____

- Would you say these improvements were a head response (items checked off on a list) or a heart response (transformed by God; lasting change)?

_____

_____

_____

_____

- How long did the improvements last? Why do you think that is?

_____

_____

_____

_____

The Magnitude of Covenant

The Power and Purpose of Lifelong Commitment

Before watching Session 2 of the DVD,
read chapters 3–4 of *Fierce Marriage*.

WATCH SESSION 2

Video Notes

As you watch the video, use the following space to take notes.

_____

_____

_____

_____

_____

_____

_____

_____

_____

_____

_____

_____

_____

_____

_____

_____

Discussion Questions

You don't really need to make a vow to stick with someone in the best of times. The inclination to run doesn't exist then. It's the low times the covenant is made for.

Matt Chandler

1. What problems might married couples encounter if they confuse love with infatuation?

_____

_____

_____

_____

_____

_____

_____

2. In Matthew 7:24, Jesus describes one house being built on sand and another being built on a rock. How might his words apply to the marriage relationship?

_____

_____

_____

_____

_____

_____

_____

3. In Genesis 1:28, God blesses the couple he has created and says to them, "Be fruitful and multiply and fill the earth and subdue it, and have dominion over the fish of the sea and over the birds of the heavens and over every living thing that moves on the earth." What does it mean to be *fruitful* in marriage (see also John 15:4 and Gal. 5:22–23)?

_____

_____

_____

_____

4. God also tells the first couple to multiply. Obviously, part of this command refers to having children. But in what ways can you and your spouse be committed to *spiritual* multiplication?

_____

_____

_____

_____

_____

5. Finally, God tells the couple to subdue the earth. What exactly is God giving us permission to do, and what does marriage have to do with it?

_____

_____

_____

_____

6. The Lord's commands to be fruitful, multiply, and subdue the earth describe his three purposes for the marriage covenant. Why is a covenant essential if we are to flourish in our marriage relationship?

_____

_____

_____

_____

_____

7. How did Jesus personify the selfless and sacrificial nature of covenantal love?

_____

_____

_____

_____

_____

8. Husbands, how can you demonstrate selfless and sacrificial love to your wife? Wives, how can you demonstrate these attributes to your husband?

_____

_____

_____

_____

For Personal Reflection

- We mentioned three purposes of covenant love in marriage. How do you currently see these at work in your marriage?

  _____

  _____

  _____

  _____

  _____

  _____

- Is there a particular covenant purpose you struggle with? Why?

  _____

  _____

  _____

  _____

  _____

  _____

- Prior to reading chapters 3–4 and watching the video, how did you and your spouse define love?

  _____

  _____

  _____

  _____

  _____

- How has understanding God's love for you (and your spouse) challenged your previous view of love?

  _____

  _____

  _____

  _____

- Identify one or two areas where your marriage is "thirsty" and in need of more love.

  _____

  _____

  _____

  _____

Priorities and Finances

Before watching Session 3 of the DVD,
read chapters 5 and 7 of *Fierce Marriage*.

WATCH SESSION 3

Video Notes

As you watch the video, use the following space to take notes.

_____

_____

_____

_____

_____

_____

_____

_____

_____

_____

_____

_____

_____

_____

_____

_____

_____

_____

Discussion Questions

I have held many things in my hands, and I have lost them all; but whatever I have placed in God's hands, that I still possess.

Martin Luther

1. Ryan's surgery caused him and Selena to come to grips with Psalm 90:12, which says, "Teach us to number our days that we may get a heart of wisdom." How can the brevity of life enable us to gain wisdom—especially in the areas of priorities and finances?

    _____

    _____

    _____

2. Many people have a "list" view of priorities, where God is first, followed by your spouse, your children, and then others. While such a view is fine, Ryan and Selena prefer a "concentric circle" view (see below). Why might this perspective be more helpful?

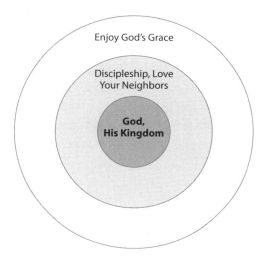

_____

_____

_____

3. In Galatians 5:1, Paul writes, "It is for freedom that Christ has set us free. Stand firm, then, and do not let yourselves be burdened again by a yoke of slavery"(NIV). How can an "ownership" perspective on finances lead to slavery?

_____

_____

_____

_____

4. In the same way, how can a "stewardship" perspective lead to freedom?

_____

_____

_____

_____

5. Ryan and Selena recommend both a "functional budget" and a "future budget." Why are both of these helpful in becoming good stewards of the resources God has given us?

_____

_____

_____

_____

6. How is your budget a reflection of what God has called you to do as a couple?

_____

_____

_____

_____

_____

7. Financial transparency is important for the health of our marriages. What are some steps you have taken—or could take—to achieve a healthy level of transparency?

_____

_____

_____

_____

_____

8. Tim Keller said that a litmus test of whether we are giving generously and sacrificially is whether we *feel* it.* How might this be a helpful measure of our giving?

_____

_____

_____

_____

_____

* Tim Keller, "Radical Generosity: 2 Corinthians 9:6–15," sermon, November 10, 1991, http://download.redeemer.com/rpcsermons/stewardship/Radical_Generosity.mp3.

For Personal Reflection

- How can the concentric view of priorities challenge the way you and your spouse prioritize?

  _____

  _____

  _____

  _____

- Do you often stress about your income or expenses? Why?

  _____

  _____

  _____

  _____

- How does the idea of stewardship help or challenge you in the way you view your finances in your marriage?

  _____

  _____

  _____

  _____

- What are some areas within your finances where stewardship could take precedence?

  _____

  _____

  _____

- How would stewardship specifically affect those areas?

_____

_____

_____

_____

Communication and Conflict

Before watching Session 4 of the DVD,
read chapters 6 and 9 of *Fierce Marriage*.

WATCH SESSION 4

Video Notes

As you watch the video, use the following space to take notes.

_____

_____

_____

_____

_____

_____

_____

_____

_____

_____

_____

_____

_____

_____

_____

_____

_____

_____

_____

_____

_____

_____

_____

_____

_____

_____

_____

_____

_____

_____

_____

_____

_____

_____

_____

_____

_____

_____

_____

_____

_____

Discussion Questions

When people talk, listen completely. Most people never listen.

Ernest Hemingway

1. After surgery, Ryan's doctor intentionally left four wires in his chest in case his heart needed to be restarted. In what sense do couples have a direct line into each other's hearts?

   _____

   _____

   _____

   _____

2. Proverbs 18:21 tells us, "The tongue has the power of life and death, and those who love it will eat its fruit"(NIV). How have you seen the power of the tongue—for good and bad—in your marriage?

   _____

   _____

   _____

   _____

3. James 1:19 states, "Everyone should be quick to listen, slow to speak and slow to become angry"(NIV). Why are James's words especially important for married couples?

   _____

   _____

   _____

   _____

4. Why is it vital to realize that the point of conflict in marriage is *reconciliation*—not proving that you're right?

_____

_____

_____

_____

_____

5. Ryan and Selena recommend that couples "fight naked"— that is, without verbal weapons or self-protective armor. How do weapons and armor run counter to the ultimate goal of reconciliation?

_____

_____

_____

_____

_____

6. Why are absolute statements, such as "you never" or "you always," counterproductive in resolving conflicts?

_____

_____

_____

_____

_____

7. It is very important to have mutual agreement about core issues in your marriage, such as who Jesus is and what his place is in your lives, parenting, vocation, and location (where you live). Do you think you and your spouse are in agreement about these core issues? Why or why not?

_____

_____

_____

_____

8. Sometimes, you need help from someone on the outside to resolve deeper issues in marriage. In such cases, why is it wise to seek godly counsel from others?

_____

_____

_____

_____

For Personal Reflection

- What signals do you miss with your spouse? Ask yourself, then ask each other.

_____

_____

_____

_____

_____

- How can you communicate more intentionally with your spouse?

  _____

  _____

  _____

  _____

- When your spouse offends you, what's your initial response? How is God leading you to respond?

  _____

  _____

  _____

  _____

- How has God used conflict as an opportunity to teach you?

  _____

  _____

  _____

  _____

- Do you have a community of believers to encourage and challenge you during marital discord? If not, how will you begin finding a community?

  _____

  _____

  _____

  _____

Intimacy and Sex

Experiencing Each Other to the Glory of God

Before watching Session 5 of the DVD,
read chapter 8 of *Fierce Marriage*.

WATCH SESSION 5

Video Notes

As you watch the video, use the following space to take notes.

_____

_____

_____

_____

_____

_____

_____

_____

_____

_____

_____

_____

_____

_____

_____

_____

_____

_____

Discussion Questions

Within the context of covenant love and mutual service, no amount
of passion is excessive.

Betsy Ricucci

1. What are some of the reasons God gave the gift of sex to married couples?

_____

_____

_____

_____

2. Why are candid conversations the best way to achieve a healthy sex life?

_____

_____

_____

_____

_____

3. What differing expectations might each spouse have about sex in their marriage?

_____

_____

_____

_____

_____

4. Why is transparency about past and present sexual issues vital to the marriage relationship?

_____

_____

_____

_____

5. Why are honesty, forgiveness, and love important ingredients in a transparent conversation about sex?

_____

_____

_____

_____

6. Ryan and Selena say that sex should never be shameful, degrading, or painful or require a spouse to violate their conscience. What impact could any of these have on a marriage, and why?

_____

_____

_____

_____

7. In contrast to shameful or degrading sex, how can married couples seek to have sex that is mutually edifying?

_____

_____

_____

8. In Ephesians 5:31–32, Paul writes: "'For this reason a man will leave his father and mother and be united to his wife, and the two will become one flesh.' This is a profound mystery—but I am talking about Christ and the church" (NIV). In what sense does the marriage relationship—including sex—reflect our relationship with Christ?

_____

_____

_____

_____

_____

For Personal Reflection

• How has sex with your spouse been challenging?

_____

_____

_____

_____

• How has sex been liberating and unifying?

_____

_____

_____

_____

- Review the love versus lust list in the book on page 169. Is there an area in your marriage where lust is the motivation?

  _____

  _____

  _____

  _____

- How can each of you take a step toward selfless loving and giving of yourself to the other?

  _____

  _____

  _____

  _____

Upward and Outward

Why Fighting for Your Marriage Means Fighting for the Future

Before watching Session 6 of the DVD,
read chapter 10 of *Fierce Marriage*.

WATCH SESSION 6

Video Notes

As you watch the video, use the following space to take notes.

_____

_____

_____

_____

_____

_____

_____

_____

_____

_____

_____

_____

_____

_____

_____

_____

_____

_____

_____

Discussion Questions

God gives us of the good things of this life, not only for necessity, but for delight, that we may not only serve him, but serve him cheerfully.

Matthew Henry

1. According to Ryan and Selena, what is the point of fighting for a stronger marriage?

   _____

   _____

   _____

   _____

2. Why is it important to lift our eyes from the here and now of marriage and think about *there* and *then*—our future legacy?

   _____

   _____

   _____

   _____

3. Ryan and Selena describe three tangible ways we can participate in God's work through our marriages: (a) discipling future generations, (b) building the local church, and (c) reaching our community with the gospel. How can a healthy, godly marriage impact not only your own children but also your grandchildren and further generations (see Ps. 78:5–7)?

   _____

   _____

   _____

4. In what ways can your healthy marriage build up your local church?

_____

_____

_____

_____

5. How can your marriage also have an impact beyond your local church in reaching your community and the world at large?

_____

_____

_____

_____

6. As you think back on both the book and video series *Fierce Marriage*, what are some of the ways you have been challenged and encouraged?

_____

_____

_____

_____

7. Husbands, what is one of the most significant challenges you face in building a healthier marriage?

_____

_____

_____

8. Wives, what is one key area of your marriage you feel called to strengthen?

_____

_____

_____

_____

_____

For Personal Reflection

• How does it make you feel to know that Christ is fighting for your marriage?

_____

_____

_____

_____

_____

• What larger purpose do you think God has for your marriage?

_____

_____

_____

_____

_____

- In what areas do you see God using your marriage to advance his kingdom?

  _____

  _____

  _____

  _____

- What excites you most when thinking about how God can use you?

  _____

  _____

  _____

  _____

Appendix

The Biblical Covenants

In chapter 3 of *Fierce Marriage*, we mentioned the many covenants in the Bible but didn't go into detail about them. However, Selena and I have found that it has greatly enriched, deepened, and bolstered our own marriage covenant to see it in the context of the unfolding covenants God has made with his people. Taking a grand view of God's covenantal action reveals much of his character and desire for marriage. We hope that our brief unpacking of the major biblical covenants below will encourage and challenge you as it does us.

God's Covenant with Adam

The Bible opens and immediately Jesus is actively involved. He was present for the creation of the world and of humankind: "Let us make man in *our* image, after *our* likeness" (Gen. 1:26, emphasis added). John 1:1–2 says, "In the beginning was the Word, and the Word was with God, and the Word was God. He was in the beginning with God." Christ, of course, is the Word.

Shortly after the creation account, God establishes his first covenant with Adam, humanity's representative:

And the LORD God commanded the man, saying, "You may surely eat of every tree of the garden, but of the tree of the knowledge of good and evil you shall not eat, for in the day that you eat of it you shall surely die." (Gen. 2:16–17)

Adam is given access to everything the garden has to offer with one condition: don't eat from the tree of the knowledge of good and evil. The theological term for this short exchange is the Edenic Covenant. It's a conditional promise. Adam will remain in perfect relationship with God and flourish forever as long as he never eats of the tree. If he does, he will die a physical death as well as a spiritual one. In verses immediately following, God decides that Adam needs a helper, so he creates Eve.

Woman is created from man—flesh is separated by way of removing a rib—and the two are immediately joined back together as one through covenantal bond. From one, God made two unique image bearers of himself: man and woman. They are at once separate and distinct parts, two entirely different views of the same full image of God. They are then joined together in marriage.

From that point in Genesis, we begin to see language shift toward "her husband" and "his wife." The foundation is laid and the first marriage is complete.

This first wedding between Adam and Eve established the framework for the multiplication of humankind. God's first directive is clear: "Be fruitful and multiply and fill the earth and subdue it" (1:28). It established the unique partnership between one man and one woman, together foreshadowing a greater covenant between Christ and his Bride. Through this partnership, Adam and Eve were instructed to be fruitful and multiply. The marital union is at the absolute center of family and procreation. Within marriage, children are conceived and families flourish.

God's larger story continued. As you likely know, Adam and Eve broke the covenant with God by eating of the tree. They were ejected from the garden, and their perfect relationship with God was severed by sin. By God's grace, they were able to live on and "be fruitful and multiply," but outside the garden. Their original sin stained every generation from that point forward.

As a result of the fall, God made another covenant with Adam and Eve called the Adamic Covenant. God announced that there would forever be enmity between Satan, Eve, and her children (humankind). Eve would experience pain in childbirth, Adam would labor and toil as the land was cursed with thorn and thistle. There would be a distortion of roles and disunity in marriage: "Your desire shall be contrary to your husband, but he shall rule over you" (3:16). Finally, death would now be the inevitable end of all living things. However, even amid the curses because of their sin, God provided what many call the "First Gospel"—a promise that Satan (and death) would ultimately be defeated by one of Eve's offspring. This Redeemer from Eve's "seed" would be injured in the process of conquering Satan but arise triumphant (v. 15). Of course, the promised victor is Jesus Christ himself, and his injury, the cross.

God's Covenant with Noah

Generations after Adam and Eve, the world was in chaos. Sin had corrupted all of humanity to its core: "every intention of the thoughts of his heart was only evil continually" (6:5). God hit the reset button and flooded the earth. Before doing so, God found Noah "blameless in his generation" (v. 9) and chose to establish—or continue—his covenant through him. God didn't forget his earlier promise to Adam, and Noah (a direct descendant of Eve) would be a vital part of fulfilling it. You know the rest of the story: Noah built an ark, God flooded the earth, the waters receded, and Noah stepped onto dry land with his family after a year in the ark. After Noah gave a burnt offering, God made another promise called the Noahic Covenant. This time, God promised to never again flood the earth and destroy all life: "I have set my bow in the cloud, and it shall be a sign of the covenant between me and the earth" (9:13).

We often picture a rainbow overhead while Noah and his family hold each other affectionately and look up at it against the stormy sky. Yet the sign of the rainbow is so much more than a pretty image: it's a symbol of the grace of God and a foretelling of the gospel. With the storm set behind, God's bow—a symbol of war—is pointed upward. Never again would people be the object of God's blanket wrath. Instead, he himself would bear the weight of sin and the total burden of salvation. Again, through covenant, God reminds us of his plan to redeem and save humankind through Jesus.

Are you getting a sense of how foundational these covenants are to the entire story the Bible tells? Stick with us; there's more.

God's Covenant with Abraham

Some centuries later, Abraham entered the scene and God made another covenant with him. This is called the Abrahamic Covenant, and it consists of three promises: God would give Abraham many descendants, he would give them land (Canaan), and from Abraham's descendants, humankind would be redeemed (12:1–3). As in the covenant with Noah, God alone bore the full weight of its requirements and reassured his people that a Redeemer was coming.

Abraham's family grew despite his sin and disbelief, because God kept his word. After a wild series of events, Abraham's grandson Jacob had twelve sons, including one named Joseph. He made his brothers jealous (because Jacob favored him), so they sold him to a caravan of Ishmaelites who took him to Egypt. Still, God is sovereign. Because of his God-given ability to interpret dreams, Joseph gained influence among Egyptian leadership. When famine hit Canaan, his brothers traveled to Egypt for help. There Joseph (in dramatic fashion) revealed his identity to them and appealed to Pharaoh to give them land in Egypt. Pharaoh obliged.

Abraham's family was displaced, but Joseph saw God working. He trusted that God would keep his promise by returning the family to Canaan one day: "As for you, you meant evil against me, but God meant it for good, to bring it about that many people should be kept alive, as they are today. . . . God will visit you and bring you up out of this land to the land that he swore to Abraham" (50:20, 24).

Even against all odds or convenience, God kept his promises and showed his trustworthiness through covenant. Abraham's descendants were many, their home was sure, and a Savior would one day arrive to deliver God's people from death once and for all.

The covenantal theme continues.

God's Covenant through Moses

When Jacob (now named Israel) and his family moved to Egypt, there were seventy persons in total. They had yet to become the "great nation" God had promised they would be. The family, now called Israelites, remained in Egypt for several centuries, where they "multiplied and grew exceedingly strong, so that the land was filled with them" (Exod. 1:7).

Eventually a new pharaoh took the throne and he saw the Israelites as a threat. He oppressed them by enslaving them and mandating that every male Hebrew baby be thrown into the Nile. One of those babies was named Moses. Through the bravery of his mother and sister, Moses survived Pharaoh's mandate and became the adopted son of Pharaoh's daughter.

After many years and another wild series of events, God used Moses to free the Israelites from their harsh slavery. Just as he promised, Abraham would become a great nation:

> I will take you to be my people, and I will be your God, and you shall know that I am the LORD your God, who has brought you out from under the burdens of the Egyptians. I will bring you into the land

that I swore to give to Abraham, to Isaac, and to Jacob. I will give it to you for a possession. I am the LORD. (6:7–8)

Once delivered from slavery in Egypt, the Israelites were battered and facing an empty, lifeless desert. Their bodies were weak and their faith weaker, but God's promise to his people was unchanged. He faithfully led them with a pillar of cloud by day and a pillar of fire by night. The Israelites were prone to doubt. Despite witnessing their own miraculous delivery from slavery, they constantly questioned God's plan. They longed for "simpler" times, when food was bountiful and life was relatively comfortable. They constantly forgot God's promise of a greater blessing: the land given to Abraham.

Amid their lack of faith, God established yet another covenant with his people. This time it was different. This time it was conditional. While God promised to bless them abundantly, it required something in return: obedience to God's law. This agreement is called the Old Covenant, or the Mosaic Covenant, and it began when Moses went to Mt. Sinai to receive the Ten Commandments. Its purpose was to govern Israel's behavior in order to maximize their trust in God and ensure that they would flourish. As long as they obeyed the law faithfully, God blessed them. If the people rebelled, God punished them.

While the Mosaic Covenant and its accompanying laws (outlined in the Mosaic and Levitical laws) were works-based, they didn't supersede God's earlier grace-based covenants. God's unconditional promises remained intact. Though his people repeatedly rebelled and lost faith, God never wavered in his desire, ability, or intention to fulfill the covenants he made: his people would still become a great nation, they would enter the promised land, and the Redeemer would still deliver them from death caused by sin in the garden.

After they had spent forty years wandering the desert, Joshua finally led the Israelites into Canaan—a "land flowing with milk and honey"—just as God promised. Given Israel's tendency to forget God's law and lordship, the book of Joshua opens with a stark reminder to avoid just that:

> Only be strong and very courageous, being careful to do according to all the law that Moses my servant commanded you. Do not turn from it to the right hand or to the left, that you may have good success wherever you go. (Josh. 1:7)

Now in their inherited land, the Israelites could finally put down roots and thrive. God's faithfulness had carried them through the desert and sustained them every step along the way. God did what he swore to do despite the countless times they turned away from him. Just before Joshua's death, he reminded the people to hold up their end of the promise. He compelled them to "fear the LORD and serve him in sincerity and in faithfulness" (24:14).

To this, the people responded:

> Far be it from us that we should forsake the LORD to serve other gods, for it is the LORD our God who brought us and our fathers up from the land of Egypt, out of the house of slavery, and who did those great signs in our sight and preserved us in all the way that we went, and among all the peoples through whom we passed. . . . Therefore we also will serve the LORD, for he is our God. (vv. 16–18)

Thus, the people of Israel renewed their covenant with God and served him "all the days of Joshua, and all the days of the elders who outlived Joshua and had known all the work that the LORD did for Israel" (v. 31). It was a much-needed time of rest, peace, and close relationship with God.

Do you see how much like a marriage God's relationship with Israel was? Do you see how these covenants are woven into the Bible's story and how important they are to God? That's how important your marriage covenant is.

We have another covenant to look at next.

God's Covenant with David

It didn't take long before Israel's faith began to slip. They "forgot the LORD their God and served the Baals and the Asheroth" (Judg. 3:7), and "everyone did what was right in his own eyes" (17:6), which is Bible-speak for rebellion against God's law. They broke their word and forgot their covenant; God's wrath was due.

This began a dark chapter in the story of God's people. In a few generations, they went from a time of rest and peace to a season rife with war and foreign oppression. Reading through Judges, we can see the pattern is cringeworthy: turn from God and suffer through punishment (usually by outsiders invading and raiding), turn back to God and cry out for deliverance, get delivered, repeat. The rebel-and-repent pattern continued for over three hundred years.

The people eventually begged for a king, so God appointed Saul. Many more wild events unfolded, Saul went sideways, and David was anointed as king. He, the youngest of all his brothers, was plucked from Bethlehem and chosen to be the new earthly king Israel desperately needed. He would help redeem his countrymen just as, one day, the ultimate Redeemer would rescue God's children. David was called a man after God's own heart, one who would do all his will (Acts 13:22). He was far from perfect, but God graciously made another covenant with him.

This new promise, dubbed the Davidic Covenant, was similar to God's covenant with Abraham. First, it was unconditional, and second, it reaffirmed redemption for God's people through the line of David (a descendant of Abraham):

> When your days are fulfilled to walk with your fathers, I will raise up your offspring after you, one of your own sons, and I will establish his kingdom. He shall build a house for me, and I will establish his throne forever. (1 Chron. 17:11–12)

In hearing God's promise, David erupted with worship! He said,

There is none like you, O LORD, and there is no God besides you, according to all that we have heard with our ears. And who is like your people Israel, the one nation on earth whom God went to redeem to be his people, making for yourself a name for great and awesome things, in driving out nations before your people whom you redeemed from Egypt? And you made your people Israel to be your people forever, and you, O LORD, became their God. (vv. 20–22)

David had already experienced firsthand the faithfulness of God and the trustworthiness of his Word. As a kid, he had slain Goliath with nothing more than a rock and a prayer! David understood more than anyone the power of being in covenant with the Almighty, and he was overjoyed. His position with God was secure, and he knew nothing would ever change that.

The New Covenant through Christ

Fast-forward a few centuries; enter a baby. In the tiny town of Bethlehem, just as promised, our Redeemer—Jesus Christ—was born. He lived the perfect life we couldn't live and died the gruesome death we should have died to pay the price for our sin and forever reconcile us to God. Just as blood sacrifices were required to atone for sin under the Old Covenant, Christ's blood is the only sacrifice sufficient to cover the sin of humanity for all time.

Jesus himself is the final promise—the New Covenant—that God made to his people. The birth, life, death, and resurrection of Jesus Christ brought us into the unprecedented period of grace we currently enjoy. By God's grace we have seen the repeated promises of a Redeemer fulfilled in the gospel. We can experience the immense joy David felt that day; when we are in Christ, God's love is unconditional, inexhaustible, and unwavering—it will never change. Jesus Christ—the "Son of David"—is on his throne forever, and the house he built is within the hearts of all believers through the gift and indwelling of the Holy Spirit.

God's faithfulness is clear, as evidenced through his various covenants with his people. It is God's nature to keep his word, the crescendo of which is in Christ—the Living Word of God.

The Culmination of God's Covenant

The end of the Bible climaxes with an eternal, perfect union of Christ and his Bride, where "he will wipe away every tear from their eyes" (Rev. 21:4). At this moment, the full New Covenant promised in Christ will at last be fulfilled. The same verse continues, "death shall be no more, neither shall there be mourning, nor crying, nor pain anymore."

The story concludes as the ultimate protagonists—the Bride (the church, believers) and the Lamb (Jesus)—are united in one final wedding. In this ultimate union all will be made new, there will be eternal celebration, and we will be finally united with our Bridegroom. Certainly, if there are tears at this wedding they will be tears of joy! "Come, I will show you the Bride, the wife of the Lamb" (v. 9).

Just as the first of God's people are sealed with covenantal promises, our final union with Christ is called a marriage. Throughout history and into eternity, God operates through covenantal promise. He proves his love to us by giving his word and keeping it, many times, despite the rebellion of his people.

This type of love is impossible for us to grasp. It's *too* sacrificial, *too* relentless, *too* unconditional. We will never know love as God knows love—at least, not on this side of eternity. Maybe we'd obey perfectly if we did, but we don't. We're a fallen, sinful, and rebellious people prone to pride. Like the Israelites, we quickly forget the promises God made to us and his faithfulness in keeping them. We can witness his miracles and still grow doubtful. We are thick in the head and fast in the feet, hard of hearing and quick to seek other gods. That will always be the case until we are fully redeemed in Christ through glorious union with him. Until then, we have lots to learn about God's covenantal love and sufficiency.

That's the primary reason God structures marriage as a covenant. Your marriage is designed to help you more meaningfully understand the covenantal promises and unconditional love of God. Your difficulty in marriage and struggles with sin and forgiveness are redeemed within marriage to bring you closer to him. And marriage is one of God's major tools for teaching you the true depths of his unending love, forgiveness, mercy, and grace.

Ryan and Selena Frederick created FierceMarriage.com in 2013 when they felt God calling them to share, with brutal transparency, the struggles he had helped them overcome. Since then, FierceMarriage .com has grown into a thriving online community with more than 200,000 unique visitors each month who generate more than 1,000,000 page views. Their social media presence is vibrant and growing, with more than 437,000 active fans and followers. Ryan also owns and manages emg, a marketing and web development company specializing in book launch marketing and programming. Ryan and Selena have two daughters and live in Tacoma, Washington.

PUT CHRIST AT THE CENTER
OF YOUR MARRIAGE

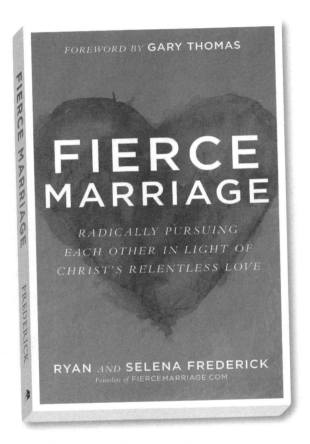

"An incredible read that will inspire, encourage, and bring hope to your relationship."

—JEFFERSON BETHKE,
New York Times bestselling author

MORE FROM
FIERCE MARRIAGE

The 31 Day Pursuit Challenge Bundle offers a gospel-centered, practical path toward loving your spouse well.
Will you take the challenge?

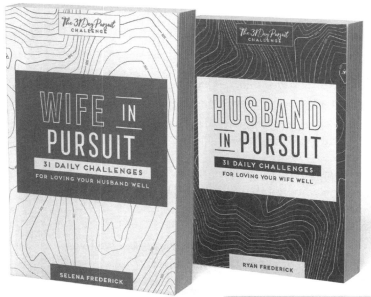

Draw closer to God and your spouse through 30 daily devotions, each one brought to life with imagery and practical application.

LIKE THIS
BOOK?
Consider sharing it with others!

- Share or mention the book on your social media platforms. Use the hashtag **#FierceMarriage**.

- Write a book review on your blog or on a retailer site.

- Pick up a copy for friends, family, or strangers— anyone who you think would enjoy and be challenged by its message!

- Share this message on Twitter or Facebook: **I loved #FierceMarriage by @FierceMarriage**

- Recommend this book for your church, workplace, book club, or class.

- Follow Baker Books on social media and tell us what you like.

 Facebook.com/ReadBakerBooks

 @ReadBakerBooks